SEVEN QUESTIONS FOR SUCCESS

Generic Improved Framework for Thinking

Colonel Mark Faulkner

Fisher King Publishing

Copyright © Mark Faulkner 2020

SEVEN QUESTIONS FOR SUCCESS

ISBN 978-1-913170-62-2

Published by

Fisher King Publishing
The Studio
Arthington Lane
Pool in Wharfedale
LS21 1JZ
England

www.fisherkingpublishing.co.uk

Colonel Mark Faulkner was educated at Ampleforth College and The Royal Military Academy Sandhurst in 1975. He served 34 years in the Army. He commanded the Royal Dragoon Guards (1994 - 1997) in Paderborn Germany, Belfast Northern Ireland and Tidworth Hampshire. He held five training appointments, the last of which was Chief of Staff Land Warfare Centre in Warminster (2004 - 2006) where he helped coordinate the Land Warfare training, both Individual and Collective, in UK and worldwide on behalf of the Director General Training Support.

After a final post in the MOD Mark left the Army in 2009. He then took up an appointment as Head of Carlton Lodge Activity Centre near Thirsk for North Yorkshire Youth Ltd, a post he held for ten years and is now the Development Manager, North Yorkshire Youth.

With thanks to...

Professor Panos Louvieris who showed me the value of the concept of 7 Questions as a framework for planning and problem solving across any business or personal situation.

Brigadier Nigel Aylwin-Foster and Major Nick Thomas who supported me when I developed the concept of 7 Questions for the Army's planning process.

My wife, Deborah, for her forbearance and encouragement during the writing of this book.

Foreword

It is my pleasure to write the foreword for an exceptional book, written by an equally exceptional author, Colonel Mark Faulkner.

The Generic Improved Framework for Thinking (GIFT) brings a practical and user friendly approach to the discipline of thinking for planning and general problem solving. The GIFT is a very accessible, seven questions scaffold for thinking that enhances decision making by increasing the comprehensibility and manageability of the decision maker in order to deal with the problem at hand i.e. think of the GIFT as an invisible guiding hand for navigating and dealing with the issues and challenges of the business environment.

The GIFT first came to my attention fifteen years ago. I was then the Director of the Surrey University Defence Technology Centre where I led the work on AI-enabled Smart Decision Support Systems for Command and Control. I immediately saw the point of the GIFT and incorporated it into the research programme with successful uptake of the outputs of the project by the customer. The GIFT has guided my thinking, as a general approach, for the development of successfully funded research proposals over the years. Moreover, I continue to use the GIFT in my current research as Co-Director of the Trusted Open Models Institute at the STFC's Hartree Centre and Director of the Digital Economy & Cyber Security Research Group in the Department of Computer Science at Brunel University London for planning, management and governance purposes. I have not looked back.

The pedigree of the GIFT is grounded in the insights that Mark gained from his experience of employing it to resolve complex adaptive problems in both his industrious defence and business careers. Moreover the requirement for the GIFT decision making approach has never been

"... the GIFT becomes a powerful communication tool facilitating shared vision and understanding for a powerful comprehensive approach to business planning and problem solving."

so important, in unprecedented times such those within which we find ourselves at the time of writing, with the COVID-19 silent assassin, to deal with the surprises, understand and prioritise the threats that expose business vulnerabilities; including, working out what direction and controlling actions must be implemented in order to achieve the desired effects for the protection of business, the economy and people.

Mark's excellent book provides a structured approach for thinking using the GIFT. When shared amongst colleagues or used within a team the GIFT becomes a powerful communication tool facilitating shared vision and understanding for a powerful comprehensive approach to business planning and problem solving. I recommend Mark's book unreservedly to you.

Professor Panos Louvieris

Brunel University London | College of Engineering Design and Physical Sciences
Department of Computer Science | Uxbridge, United Kingdom

Contents

CHAPTER 1

WHAT IS THIS BOOK ABOUT?

This book aims to provide a framework for thinking and an approach for planning, problem solving and decision making. The Generic Improved Framework for Thinking (GIFT) is not a process but simply a logical and structured approach that will serve you and those around you in any situation that you may face. It can be applied intuitively or deliberately because it is simple and adaptable. It is a default for when you think to yourself 'how do I deal with this?' or 'where do I start?' It helps as a focus for collaborative planning and for achieving integration of functional areas in a team. It is a concept that supports both leadership and management.

Every day all of us face problems that require us to make plans, make decisions and to implement plans. During the implementation we may need to adjust our plans and make more decisions. Often we do this intuitively and give little thought to our approach. Our thinking will be governed by a whole range of qualities, characteristics and experiences that will impact on our thoughts and ideas. The picture below captures some of the influences on our thinking and these will be different for every person:

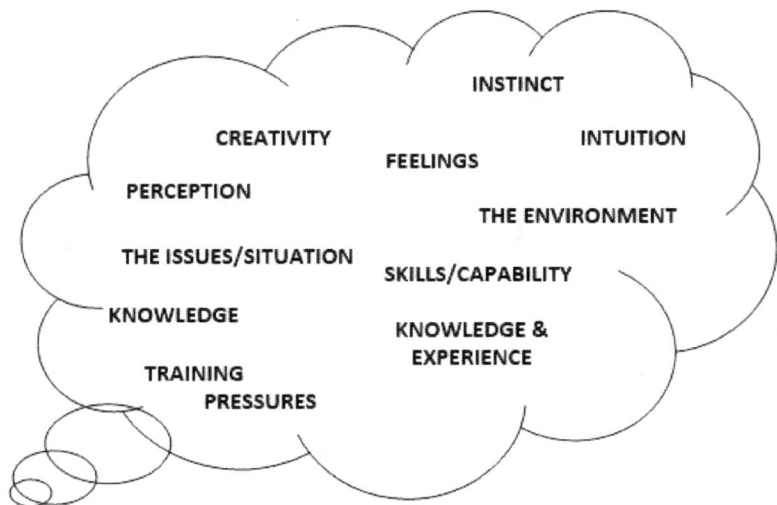

INSTINCT

CREATIVITY   INTUITION

FEELINGS

PERCEPTION

THE ENVIRONMENT

THE ISSUES/SITUATION   SKILLS/CAPABILITY

KNOWLEDGE   KNOWLEDGE &
EXPERIENCE

TRAINING
PRESSURES

IDEAS...

Illustration 1

Sometimes we can solve relatively simple problems individually because we have the experience, training or confidence so to do. However, in more complex or unfamiliar situations we may need to call on the help of colleagues, professionals, a friend, a neighbour, or a member of our family. Once a task has been done successfully once or twice, it goes into the memory bank and the solution or approach can be repeated intuitively later. In more deliberate situations, such as producing a strategic plan you will need to draw on the experience and expertise of your team; it is important to involve them in the planning to ensure that they make their contribution to the solution, buy in to the plan and feel valued.

WHY SHOULD I READ THIS BOOK?

The questions below will focus your mind on the potential value to you of this book:

- Have you ever struggled to know where to start when faced with a problem?

- When you are leading a team in planning and decision making, how do you get the functional teams to contribute to the achievement of the common goal?

- How do you integrate the actions of functional teams or different parts of your business and avoid them working in silos?

- Do you and the members of your planning team approach planning, problem solving and decision making in the same way?

- Are you always clear in your own mind why you have adopted a certain course of action and have the implications of your decision been thought through?

- Do you feel when making a plan with your planning team that your collective approach is precise, organised and disciplined?

If you do not feel confident in answering these questions positively, the GIFT will help you and those working for you.

WHAT IS THE GENERIC IMPROVED FRAMEWORK FOR THINKING (GIFT)?

The GIFT is an approach to planning, decision making and problem solving, based on addressing 7 Questions in 3 Stages. It is outcome and effect oriented and it has a strong focus on purpose.

The 3 Stages. Problem solving, planning and decision-making will be initiated by the occurrence of a situation or deliberately by direction or a vision given by a superior. The situation or direction sets the thinking in context.

Stage 1 - The What and the Why?

Q1. What are the issues and obstacles and why?

Q2. What must I achieve and why?

Q3. What changes/outcomes are needed to resolve the issues and what direction must I give, and information must be gathered, to enable the development of a plan?

Stage 2 – Analysis:

- Conducting analysis, required research and gathering Information in accordance with the direction given.

- Findings should be briefed to the planning team before proceeding with the planning at Stage 3.

Stage 3 - The How?

Q4. Where in the business environment can I best achieve the actions/changes/outcomes?

Q5. What assets do I need to accomplish each action/changes/outcomes?

Q6. When and where in time and space do the actions/changes/outcomes need happen in relation to each other?

Q7. What Governance measures do I need to impose?

Several people have remarked that this is just the 'who, what, when, why, where and how. They are right to an extent. However, the GIFT puts those adverbs and pronouns into a logical order that should guide thinking during problem solving and planning.

WHAT ARE THE ORIGINS OF THE CONCEPT?

What shaped my thinking in the development of the GIFT and why questions?

The journey that led to the development of the 7 Questions started in February 1997. Having completed two and a half years commanding the Royal Dragoon Guards, a regiment of about 500 personnel, normally equipped with tanks and other armoured vehicles, I was posted to the Command and Staff Trainer (North) in Catterick as its commander. The job entailed setting scenarios to practise commanders and their staff in developing plans and then playing out their plans against an enemy force using a constructive simulation in order to facilitate leadership and team development through assessment, analysis and coaching. I had a team of subject matter experts from all the elements that make up a task organised force. We had to identify good practice and areas that required education, learning and development for individuals within the team and collectively as a group. The experience of coaching over a hundred teams through planning, decision making and the execution of plans, provided an opportunity to observe individuals planning and executing plans in a wide spectrum of situations, from small teams dealing with relatively simple situations to large teams dealing with complex situations and deciding how to deploy their resources in order to accomplish their missions.

I learned much from the experience of coaching people who often knew more than I or my staff, who were often more senior and some who did not welcome our comments and advice. I learned that to make sure that these groups left us after 5 days better for the experience of the training we put them through, we, as a team of coaches, had to help our customers to take ownership of their own development. We had to analyse, coach and mentor, not assess and criticise if we were to be successful.

The following bullets are a summary of observations that were common to many of the teams passing through or to put it another way the issues that we had to address to help develop the teams passing through our hands: You may recognise some of these traits in your own teams, whether you are the leader or a member of a team.

- Planning in stove pipes or silos. Individuals went through the process of planning from their own perspective, concentrating on making plans for their area of expertise, without giving due consideration to integrating their contribution with the work being done in the other functional areas. They were in their comfort zone. The challenge for the leader was how to integrate the separate elements of the team working towards, and contributing to, the achievement of a common goal.

- Focus on the 'how?' before gaining a clear understanding of the 'what and the why?' There is a natural tendency when faced with a problem to want to get to the solution as fast as possible. A whole range of thoughts will go through the mind drawing on past experiences that can result in 'jumping to conclusions'. We have all been there and can be tempted to rush in to problem solving through trial and error rather than disciplined analysis. Think about why DIY always takes three times longer than one initially thinks or putting together a flat packed piece of furniture before reading the instructions and getting together the right tools for the job. In the end rushing in without a clear understanding of the 'what and the why' wastes time and leads to frustration; in the worst case it can lead to making false assumptions which become very difficult to pull back from even when it becomes obvious that they turn out to be wrong. This is amplified in the film 'a Bridge Too Far' www.youtube.com/watch?v=AWL184ZcSxA

- Failure to take early account of the obstacles to the achievement of the mission/goal or vision before making a plan. For military people this means the enemy and the other players in the contemporary operating environment. For businesses it means the competition, the market place, the customer and the business environment and conditions. In a situation such as a road crash the obstacles could include the traffic, the injuries to people involved, the danger of fire and the safety of those helping to resolve the situation.

- Process driven planning. Processes are useful tools to help answer questions and address specific issues. They provide invaluable support to analysis. Processes should therefore be used to support the analysis required in problem solving but not to drive it. There is nothing wrong with process per se; problems arise when team's or individual's thinking is driven by trying to rearrange thoughts to meet the requirements of the process. I came to the conclusion that process is most useful where it helps to answer a question. The question provides the focus and purpose for the work.

THE USE OF QUESTIONS AS THE FOCUS

Why have I used questions as the basis of the framework?

The seed for the use of questions developed as I experimented with finding more effective ways of coaching and mentoring to avoid the confrontation that resulted from what could be viewed as criticism. By asking individuals what they were doing and how their work contributed to the overall plan, and drawing the audience on with appropriate supplementary questions, I found that opportunities to coach through making suggestions and opening free and open dialogue led to constructive engagement and development. People found questions a very helpful way to focus the work that they had to do; they found the approach really useful and not threatening. At the time I was studying for a diploma in performance coaching and was introduced to Neuro Linguistic Programming and came across the following on the power of questions:

Questions:

- Arouse interest and encourage thinking

- Focus attention on particular areas

- Empower people to access their own knowledge, resources and experiences

- Make people curious and lead to other questions

- Ultimately, questions demand an answer

Thus over a period of time we (I with my staff) began to develop those questions that everyone involved in the planning process needed to address, in varying levels of detail and from their own subject matter perspective, in order to make their contribution to the development of the plan. Initially the questions were quite lengthy and detailed. However, it became clear to us that it was best to keep the questions really simple so that they became a start point for all people in all situations and could then be tailored and expanded depending on the complexity of the problem and the analysis required in producing answers that would contribute to the plan. This realisation was a really important driver when the 7 Questions were being taught. The end result was a framework for thinking and an approach, not a new process. Does any of this ring true for you? If so the GIFT may help you.

MY INTENT

My intent in writing this book is to draw on my observations of people operating in a team, their interactions, the lessons that I gained from my experiences and the simple principles and disciplines necessary to plan, solve problems and make decisions. I will provide examples from my own experience from my 34 years in the Army, in the work that I have done with the University of Surrey and a number of businesses and Service organisations and more recently from my current job for North Yorkshire Youth Ltd, as head of an outdoor education and development centre. My purpose is to enable you to think about how you might adapt the concept to serve your purpose as an individual, a team member or as a leader.

DEDUCTIONS

You will have made some deductions in your own mind when reading the first few pages and will be forming an opinion about whether to read on and explore further, or to put this book back on the shelf. Your deductions will have been influenced by the subconscious (or adaptive unconscious) and conscious elements shown in Illustration 1. You will be making a decision dependant partly on why you picked this book up in the first place. I hope that I have whetted your appetite sufficiently to help you to decide to read on in order to explore further how the GIFT might apply to your situation. I have called the framework the GIFT, the Generic Improved Framework for Thinking. It is generic and adaptable to different organisations and situations; it would be presumptuous of me to assume that you have no framework for thinking, but I hope that some of the ideas and disciplines that the GIFT provides will help you and those with whom you work to improve your approach; and finally it is not another process, it is a framework to help you to bring precision, organisation and discipline to your thinking when conducting planning and decision making.

CHAPTER 2

THE UNDERPINNING UNDERSTANDING
REQUIRED TO EXPLOIT THE APPROACH

This chapter aims to provide the understanding that underpins my proposed approach to planning, decision making and day to day problem solving. This understanding may influence leaders in considering any changes in behaviour required to develop their organisation and its people. I intend to raise areas that readers might like to compare to their own approach to leadership, ways of working and ways of getting the best out of their own people.

First of all I will give you my understanding of empowerment which draws on the military doctrine of 'Mission Command'.   My experience is that people respond very positively to being given a feeling that they are making a real contribution to the team and the success of that team. We all like to feel involved and valued. The challenge is to understand the fundamentals of real empowerment and how to apply them:

- Team leaders need to understand their leader's intent, their own contribution to that intent and the wider context of what the organisation is trying to achieve.

- They need to be clear on the outcome that they are required to achieve and how it contributes to the achievement of the common goal.

- They need to have been provided with sufficient assets/resources to achieve the required outcome.

- The leader must impose the minimum number of governance measures, so as not unnecessarily to constrain the freedom of action of his/her team leaders.

- Team leaders are able to decide how to achieve the desired outcomes within the freedoms allowed to them and the constraints imposed.

Let me expand on some of the ideas introduced above:

- Expression of Intent: the expression of a number of contributory actions each carried out to result in a change in the current situation or outcome, each with its own contributory purpose, which when combined, integrated and synchronized will achieve the overall purpose. This thinking is very cleverly captured in 'The Goal' by Eliyahu M. Goldratt and Jeff Cox. This is a novel with a very clear business message. A statement of intent drawn from the theme of this book could be; 'I am going to install robots into my factory in order to reduce the requirement for people working 24 hours. I am going to examine how best to use the robots in my production line to speed up the manufacture of those items I need to make in order to meet my orders on time. I will exploit the use of robots in order to increase my profits through meeting my orders more quickly and thereby increasing the throughput of what I can produce. This will result in the achievement of my overall mission 'to save the division from closure by turning it from a loss making to a profitable part of the company'. Note that each action has a purpose and that the sum of the individual actions contributes to the overall goal – to make a profit.

- Governance. Targets are often are used to 'govern' the efforts of an organisation or team. Targets are only valuable if they are each set in order to achieve well defined purposes that contribute to the achievement of the mission. To test a target, the effect of the target on actions and outcomes need to be considered if the law of unexpected consequences is to be mitigated. Arrest targets imposed on the police in the early 2000s led to police being driven to arrest anyone seen to be infringing the letter of the law, rather than making arrests in order to bring serious criminals to justice. Bad targets without a clearly defined purpose can unnecessarily restrict freedom of action resulting in wasting resources and diverting attention from the overriding purpose of an organisation. There are too many examples of targets imposed by governments that prove counter productive and go against the philosophy of empowerment.

- Outcome: an outcome is a result, or change, achieved as a consequence of an action or a series of actions. All actions must be designed to have an effect which supports the overall purpose and the desired outcome. If they do not, then review them. A common symptom of poor decision making is a failure to analyse in enough detail the implications of a course of action, i.e. to test it against the issues that you are addressing and the wider context. It is fine to consciously take a risk in the knowledge of a possible negative impact, as long as mitigating actions are considered should the negative effect begin to occur.

- Assets: actions require assets or resources to achieve the desired outcome. These include equipment, people, training, estate, spares, power supply, finance to meet operating and investment costs and so on. If a course of action is not properly resourced across all its contributing functions a risk is being taken. As I stated above, taking a risk is fine as long as it is consciously taken, it is monitored and contingency plans are developed if the risk becomes reality.

- Governance: governance is essential to control and coordinate the implementation of a plan. But over control gives a message of lack of trust in employees. People respond to responsibility and a feeling of being trusted. But trust can only be built on mutual understanding of the intent and of the capabilities of a person or a team. The more experienced and competent the team, the less the need for control measures. But governance is important to ensure synchronisation and integration of contributory actions and to monitor progress by time and space.

FUNDAMENTAL INGREDIENTS OF SUCCESS

In observing the behaviours and interactions of teams in planning, decision-making and the execution of their plans, it became apparent to me that there were various ingredients that were essential for a team to be successful. A paradigm for an effective team could look like this:

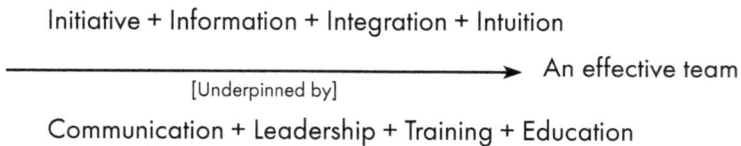

Initiative + Information + Integration + Intuition
$$\xrightarrow{\hspace{5cm}} \text{An effective team}$$
[Underpinned by]
Communication + Leadership + Training + Education

Looking at the ingredients more closely:

INITIATIVE

- To gain competitive advantage, it is necessary to take and retain the initiative in the marketplace. Therefore throughout planning and its implementation:

- Think competition, monitor the competition, be proactive not reactive. Gaining and maintaining the initiative is a critical ingredient in any competitive activity. Also denying the initiative to the opposition is equally important.

- The key to gaining and keeping the initiative was captured by a US Air Force Colonel, in what is known as the Boyd Cycle or the Decision Cycle.

Decision Cycle

The elements of the decsion cycle are:

- ➢ **Observe**

- ➢ **Orientate**

- ➢ **Decide**

- ➢ **Act**

- During the Korean War Colonel Boyd, a US Air Force Colonel, studied performance records of engagements between Russian MIG jets flown by the Chinese with those of less advanced American aircraft flown by USAF pilots. The latter invariably gained superiority in air combat, but why given their inferior planes?

- Put quite simply, American pilots could see more of what was going on around them because their aircraft had bigger canopies affording the pilots much better visibility of the skies. The American aircraft may have been inferior in some ways but their pilots could see much more of what was going on and thus anticipate better than their enemy. The quality of the resultant decision making gave them a combat advantage; they were able to observe, orientate, decide and act faster than their enemy.

- During planning, and as plans are implemented, it is necessary to observe (recognize the Situation) in order to identify/monitor opportunities and threats; orientate in order to analyse information and the situation and to develop options, decide on a chosen course of action and act faster than the competition.

- It is worth reflecting at this stage that the OODA functions are human functions that can be supported and speeded up, or even replaced with technology. The cycle starts with Observe or gathering information on the situation...

- See https://en.wikipedia.org/wiki/John_Boyd_(military_strategist)

INFORMATION

Information is the life blood of decision making. The challenge is to be clear on what you know and what you need to know. In order to get the information that you need for your business, it is essential to establish your information requirements - i.e. the information that you need to develop your strategy, to confirm that your plan remains on track and to monitor the reaction of the competition, market place and customers to what you are doing. Your eyes and ears in the business environment are all your employees and particularly your sales staff; the worldwide web is the electronic equivalent. If all your people know the information requirements and the reason why the information is important to your plan, then they can all contribute to maintaining situational awareness and understand the significance to your plan of information acquired,.

During planning it is inevitable that assumptions and judgments have to be made where the information required to take planning forward is not available. When an assumption is made, a risk is being taken. Each such risk must be recorded and continually monitored to confirm whether or not it is, and remains, valid. Monitoring assumptions and risks is critical, so that you can take early mitigating action if the situation does not develop as predicted. The information required to confirm that the assumptions remain valid are critical information requirements. If you identify that the situation that you predicted has changed, you should adjust your plan or initiate a contingency plan.

Before Operation Market Garden in 1944, it had been believed that the bridge at Arnhem was not strongly defended by the Germans. However, shortly before the operation was launched information was received through Dutch resistance and intercepted communications by General Browning that there were two Panzer Divisions in the area. He felt that it was too late to change the plan. His decision to go ahead and the fact that 30 Corps made slow progress to link up with the airborne landings led to the defeat of the airborne forces in their attempts to hold the bridge against the German counter attack.

In business it is critical to continually gain information from the customers. The customers' vision, feelings and thoughts will change. It is essential to shape your output to meet their requirements and ensure that they think yours is the organisation with the solution they seek.

After leading the market for years, IBM entered the 90s on the brink of disaster. On 1 April 1993 Lou Gerstner took over as Chief Executive. He noticed that the business had fallen into negative practices, the deleterious effects of which were not noticed. They were technological leaders with growing revenues. IBM was staffed with people who understood what computers could do but not what they could do for people. Mr Gerstner made customer contact the priority. Customers reported that they wanted solutions to their problems. Mr Gerstner changed the focus from selling hardware to selling products that bundled software with the hardware to solve customers' business problems. This change was reflected in the IBM advertisements in the mid 90s.

Do your team leaders know what assumptions that you have made and the reason for all your information requirements? If they don't, I suggest that they should in order to empower them to alert you to information, either positive or negative, that will affect your plan. Positive information can present either reassurance that the plan is on track or an opportunity, negative information may mean that a threat is developing. It should not be ignored. Rather it needs to be observed and if necessary be dealt with proactively not reactively. Your decision cycle is continually fed by information and is the enabler for orientation, decision and action. Hence all staff must know what to look for and what information you may be interested in and why. Schulz in a cartoon strip shows two vikings looking up at a crow's nest toward a crewmate who had been sent aloft. The captain says, 'Do you see anything up there?' The answer from above was 'Yes, I see a lot of crow droppings.' This exchange highlights the importance of your people needing to understand the purpose of the information that you want them to gather or keep an eye on.

INTEGRATION

Integration and synchronization result in the achievement of synergy. General Patton, the bombastic and charismatic US 2nd World War commander summed up this point in what he called the Musicians from Mars:

"There is still a tendency in each separate unit to be a one handed puncher. By that I mean the rifleman wants to shoot, the tanker wants to charge, the artilleryman to fire. That is not the way to win battles. If the band played a piece first with the piccolo, then with the brass horn, then with the clarinet, and then with the trumpet, there would be a hell of a lot of noise but no music. To get harmony in music each instrument must support the other. Team play wins. You musicians of mars... must come into the concert at the proper place and at the proper time."

MAJ GEN George S. Patton jr. 1941

So whatever your business you should make sure that the actions of the functional areas are both integrated and synchronized. Each area needs to know its contribution to the business goals and objectives and when its actions need to take place in relation to the others in time and space. So what are the functional areas in your business that need to be integrated and synchronized? The table below aims to illustrate the idea.

TIME	Q1/08	Q2/08	Q3/08	Q4/08	Q1/09
ACTIONS	DEVELOP	TEST	PREPARE	MANU.	LAUNCH
OUTPUT/OBJECTIVE					
PREDICTED COMPETITION/ CUSTOMER ACTION/REACTION					
RESEARCH & DEVELOPMENT					
MANUFACTURE					
MARKETING					
SALES					
CUSTOMER SERVICES					
HR					
DISTRIBUTION					
FINANCE & ACCOUNTING					
DECISIONS					

The table above sets the actions of each of the functions of a business in the context not only of the other functions but relates those actions in time with the outputs that are planned to be achieved and the predicted action / reaction of the competition and the customers. The final row is for decisions that will need to be taken at each stage, such as go or no go; if information indicates that any of the planned actions are either ahead or behind schedule or if information from the monitoring of the competition poses a threat, then decisions will need to be taken on how the plan must be adjusted.

All the elements in the table interact and are inter-related; they are also dynamic. To maintain efficiency and effectiveness the elements need to be kept in harmony and where harmony is threatened action needs to be taken. So, for example, if it is identified that the competition is discovered to be launching a similar product at the same time, options need to be decided to mitigate the threat and retain the initiative.

INTUITION

The dictionary definition of intuition is *'the ability to know or understand something by using your feelings rather than by considering the facts'*. It is the product of education, training and experience. Instinct is *'a natural tendency to behave in a particular way using the knowledge and abilities that someone was born with rather than thought or training'*. There is a place for both in developing a vision, a conceptual intent and in hasty decision making. Both should be encouraged in members of a team especially when considering Stage 1 (Questions 1 -3). The ideas can be tested and developed in Stage 2, the analysis. In hasty decision making, leaders may have to go with their gut feelings. In deliberate decision making there is still a place for intuition and instinct, as long as it is backed up in its implementation by logical reasoning, analysis and planning by the leader. The power and importance of intuition is exposed and developed in 'You Have 3 Minutes' by Ricardo Bellino. This book should be on your 'must read' list and I feel is complementary to the concept of the GIFT.

In the Second World War the Chief of the Imperial General Staff, General Sir Alan Brooke, later the 1st Viscount Alanbrooke, spent much of his time discussing with Winston Churchill ways to seize the initiative. The accounts of their discussions are captured in Sir Arthur Bryant's To Turn the Tide (against the Axis powers). Churchill produced a constant stream of ideas; Alan Brooke had to assess what was achievable from a military point of view, within the context of Churchill's visionary intuition. He spent many nights in deep argument with Churchill dissuading him against his more outrageous ideas, while seeking the gem of genius that would stand a chance of success and then lead in the development of a successful strategy. All this he had to do within the power politics of both politicians and military commanders. This illustrates the balance of intuition and instinct with detailed analysis and planning with which successful leaders and their chiefs of staff must grapple.

COMMUNICATIONS

Leaders at every level must communicate their plans to their teams in a way that those who are involved in its implementation clearly understand their contribution to the implementation of the plan and the overall output. They must feel that even if they are only one small cog in the overall system, their contribution is nonetheless important and valuable, and why it is.

Before the battle of Austerlitz in December 1805, when Napoleon's 68.000 troops faced 90,000 better equipped forces of Russia and Austria, Napoleon rode 30 miles speaking to his troops, explaining his plan and the critical nature of their contribution to a successful outcome. Austerlitz was one of Napoleon's greatest victories and demonstrates the power of communication in motivating those charged with the execution of a plan.

In the information age communication is faster and reaches more people. One of the key challenges for leaders today is how to exploit the different means of communication and how to protect the business against the competition's use of communication. Networks are made up of humans, information systems and communication systems. Each has its strengths and weaknesses which need to be understood.

Observe

Act — Network — Orientate

Decide

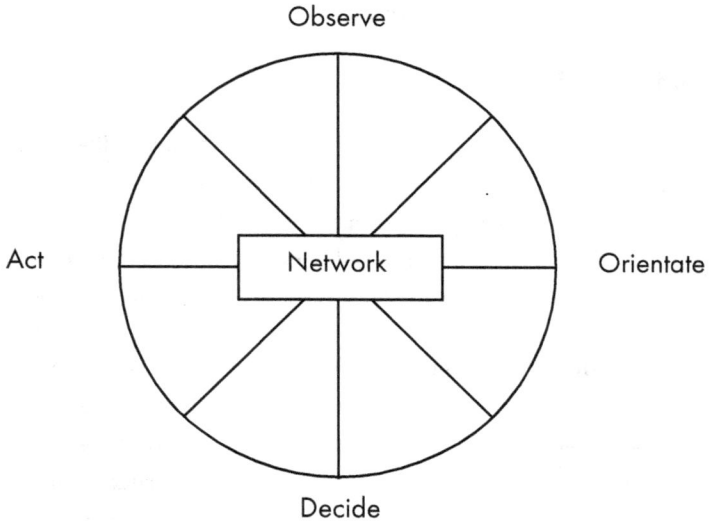

Illustration 2

The illustration above shows how the OODA functions are all interlinked by the passage of information through the network. Creating a communications plan that connects those members of the staff involved in managing and leading each of these areas is critical to keeping the plan on track during implementation. Hence the need for them to understand the broader context of what they have been directed to do in support of the plan.

LEADERSHIP

The leader of a team engaged in planning, problem solving and decision making will determine how the members of the team interact with him/her and the other members. Below are a number of lessons drawn from observations from my time spent watching team dynamics and from working for different leaders which aims to provide food for thought for leaders and managers:

- Clarity of Thought and Purpose. The leaders with clarity of thought and purpose do not allow their minds to be cluttered by unnecessary detail. The clarity is in knowing in which direction they want to move the business forward and why. They also provide clarity of intent throughout planning and the implementation of the plan, especially when the situation changes. The converse is when leaders do not trust their subordinates and intervene when they do not need to. The military refer to this type of behaviour as the long screwdriver. Of course there may be a need to intervene when things are going wrong and subordinates cannot cope, but to do so when they are meeting the intent in their own way breaks down trust and stifles initiative.

- Inclusiveness and Listening. The most effective leaders that I have served and observed are those that engage with their staff and involve them in the planning process. Engagement requires a leader to listen to the ideas of the team; to decide what to explore further and what to discard; and to judge when decisions and direction are required to keep the planning moving forward.

- Risk Taking. The leader must decide the level and detail of risk taking. Taking risk blindly is a recipe for disaster. Risks can be taken both in what is to be done, and why, when the purpose needs to be clear and the likely obstacles and implications clearly understood; or in the resources or assets allocated to achieving an outcome. Where a risk is taken, it needs to be defined, monitored and mitigated against. Information that will indicate whether or not the risk is paying off needs to be recorded as information requirements and communicated to those who might find or come across the information.

- Empowerment. It is much more rewarding to work in an organisation where empowerment is practised not just talked about. In a management team it is highly beneficial to have middle mangers that are prepared to take responsibility and to take the lead for problem solving during the implementation of a plan. This requires middle managers to feel empowered and trusted and for them to have a clear understanding of their boss's intent, and in particular the outcomes/effects required. It is much easier to rein back an over-zealous middle manager than to have middle managers who are reactive not proactive. Setting the conditions for such a culture requires leaders at every level to have a clear knowledge of the plan, the obstacles that have to be overcome and the boss' decision criteria; i.e. the information/situation that will require a decision, an understanding of the level of freedom delegated and excellent lines of communication upwards, downwards and sideways. Empowerment needs to be regulated by governance measures that do not unnecessarily restrict freedom of action. The measures imposed are dependent on the experience and capability of each manager and the level of risk being taken.

- Decision Making. Decisive, timely and confidence/belief when imparting a decision is critical in inspiring confidence.

The way in which the tips above could be implemented will depend on the style and personality of leaders and may manifest themselves in different ways. There is no blueprint for what will make a successful leader. My aim in this book is to provide leaders with some generic tools to help structure their thinking and assist them in applying leadership at any level and in any situation. Hence the GIFT should be seen as a management and leadership tool that focuses more on the 'what and the why' rather than the 'how'.

TRAINING AND EDUCATION

I was once invited to present to a seminar on Education and Training in the Army for the Digital Era. My first thought was to define the difference between training and education. I looked up 'education' in the Oxford Dictionary of Quotations and extracted the following:

> 'Education is what survives when what has been learned has been forgotten'. The New Scientist 1964

The quotation struck me as particularly important. Education puts training and learning in context. It provides the broader understanding that underpins our approach to a situation. Training provides the skills required for the functions that are required of the people in a business. Training needs therefore to be relevant and timely. Skills' fade occurs if the new skills learned are not practised immediately after the training. Skills need to be practised until they become embedded and intuitive.

It is hard to measure the impact of education and training on the efficiency and effectiveness of a workforce but my own experience leaves me in no doubt that it is huge. In the Second World War the Germans appreciated this and maintained the integrity of their training infrastructure right to the end

SUMMARY

The key messages in this chapter are the critical importance of information management in support of decision making and the benefits of empowerment with appropriate governance. That is enough of theory. The chapters that follow will look at the GIFT in action.

CHAPTER 3

HASTY/INTUITIVE PLANNING USING THE GIFT

Background

The aim of this Chapter is to show you how the GIFT supports Hasty/ Intuitive planning and decision making. When an unexpected event occurs, the first decision that has to be made is 'do I change or adjust my plan?', or perhaps more importantly 'am I prepared to take responsibility for playing my part in addressing the issues that I face?'

Preliminaries. All planning is carried out to deal with a situation. It may be that you have a plan that you are implementing when something happens that forces you to review your plan. There are at the simplest level two options:

- Do I ignore the situation and bash on with my plan regardless?

Or

- Do I review the implications of the situation and either adjust my plan or in extremis abandon it and make a new plan in the context of the new situation?

So to bring these points into sharp focus I will take you through a worked example. I intend to show you how the GIFT will help you to review the situation and to guide your thoughts as you make a plan in a situation where there is little time and you have to come to quick decisions.

In the example the GIFT is supporting you by acting as a framework for what you will think about and the decisions that you will take using your intuition.

SITUATION

You are driving your car along a fairly minor road and your intent is to get to a meeting with a client in order to discuss new business opportunities. You are meeting the client in his office and you are on track to arrive 15 minutes before the meeting in one hour's time. As you come round a corner in the road you are confronted by an accident involving a car and a light truck about two hundred metres in front of you. It looks pretty nasty, there is smoke or steam coming from the front of the car and it appears that the people involved are still in their vehicles.

In such a situation your mind will go into overdrive and your thinking will be influenced by a number of the elements shown in Illustration 1 in Chapter 1 and ideas on how to deal with this situation will be rushing through your mind. What I will show you in this worked example is how your thoughts could be ordered if you were well trained and practised in applying the logic of the 7 Questions. I accept entirely that you may have many of the thoughts almost simultaneously; but once the initial adrenalin rush is over and you have taken the immediate instinctive actions, the GIFT can provide precision, order and discipline to your thinking , when you have time to reflect on what else you need to think about to take control of the situation. During the training for operations in Northern Ireland, my instructor called this moment of reflection 'the Condor moment' from the pipe tobacco advertisement of the 1970s.

Question 1 - What are the issues and obstacles and why?

What will your immediate thoughts be? I suggest that the things that will be going through your mind in the first seconds of being confronted by the situation, in no particular order are as follows:

- What has happened here? What should I do? My meeting is really important; I don't think that I can get past this accident, but I could turn around and find another route and make the meeting on time; but hang on, there could be injuries here and it may be that nobody will come down this road soon.

- I cannot abandon these poor people because they might be in pain or in danger or worst case someone might die.

- Do not ring 999 until you are able to answer the questions the 999 operator will ask:

  - Police, Fire Brigade, Ambulance?

  - Where is the accident and are there any restrictions on the way they approach the scene?

  - How many are injured and are any of the people in a life threatening situation?

  - Is there any other immediate information you can give me?

Once you have been told the emergency services are on the way you can continue to consider the issues and how they will affect your planning on your actions and priorities.

Question 2 - What must I achieve and why?

I must take control of the situation in order to stabilize the situation until the emergency services arrive.

So change of plan. I can ring and explain to my client what happened when I have all this under control. You put on your hazard warning lights and re-position your vehicle to ensure that oncoming traffic has plenty of warning of the hazard. You then ring 999 and ask for all three emergency services – police, fire brigade and ambulance services and then make your way towards the accident site about 40 metres away, and your thoughts go back to the issues that you have to deal with.

That probably took a few seconds and it is back to square one! Just as you get out of the car someone arrives at the other side of the accident.

Did I change my plan and decide to take charge of the situation?

Having decided to be a responsible citizen and having assessed the situation and set yourself a mission you intuitively turn to the GIFT to structure your thoughts and govern your approach to making a plan.

Question 1 - What are the issues and why?

- There seems to be a risk of fire which could make the situation worse and make it dangerous for me and others.

- There may be a risk that some people will lose their lives for want of timely intervention.

- People are injured and they will need all the help that we can give them; but we must be careful not to make their injuries worse.

- Other people will be arriving and lack of control in managing the situation could lead to chaos.

Question 2 - What must I achieve and why?

I must manage the situation and do what I can to ensure the people involved are helped and as safe and reassured as possible in order to prepare for the arrival of the emergency services.

Question 3 – What objectives must I set (in the context of the issues) and what direction must I give to develop a plan?

Again this sort of thinking will come to you intuitively and the intent schematic below is illustrative of the picture that you may have in your mind. The answer to this question must be addressed from the perspective of what and why and not how in order to set the most efficient and effective conditions for addressing the how (i.e. the courses of action open- Q4-Q7). In effect doing it this way will reduce mistakes later thereby avoiding having to go back to the beginning, wasting the precious resource - time.

So in the context of the obstacles and issues you face (Q1) and an analysis of what you must do and your purpose, you formulate your 'Intent'. The Intent schematic displays the result of your thoughts in a way that makes it easy to assess the interrelationship of the objectives that you need to set.

INTENT SCHEMATIC

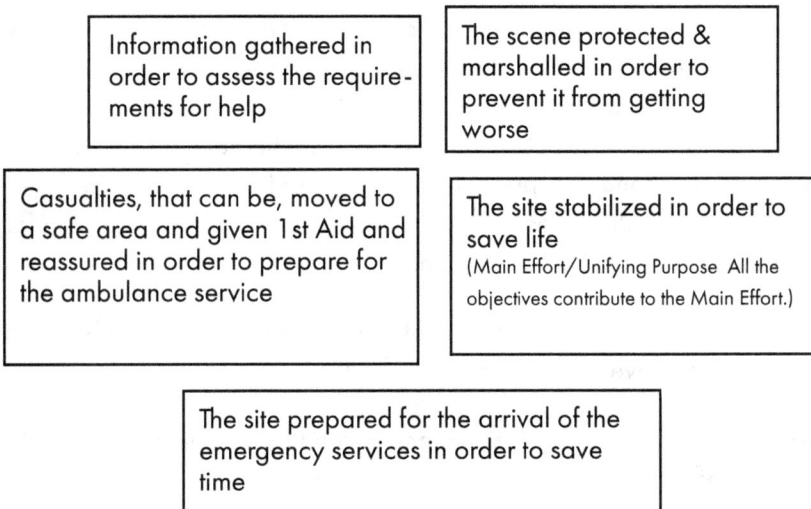

Information gathered in order to assess the require-ments for help	The scene protected & marshalled in order to prevent it from getting worse
Casualties, that can be, moved to a safe area and given 1st Aid and reassured in order to prepare for the ambulance service	The site stabilized in order to save life (Main Effort/Unifying Purpose All the objectives contribute to the Main Effort.)

The site prepared for the arrival of the emergency services in order to save time

Illustration 3

Note that the language is outcome based and describes each objective in terms of the effect and its purpose - the why. The purpose can be achieved in many different ways.

The aim of giving direction is twofold; to drive the gathering of information; and the conduct of appropriate analysis; this will inform the development of courses of action.

Direction

In this situation it may be that you are not comfortable in taking the lead and that somebody arrives who takes over the responsibility from you. However, in this case you are comfortable to be the one giving direction until the emergency services arrive. In this fast evolving situation you give instructions to people as they arrive based on your assessment of priorities. You would probably give a quick brief to the first person to arrive to tell the person that you have called 999 and the emergency services are on the way. You note that the car of the person has its 4 way flashers on and you assess that there is no danger of vehicles arriving from either direction ploughing in to the site and making the situation worse. So you give direction to the 4 people who have now arrived on what is to be done to support the emergence of a plan. They will then carry out the 7 Questions intuitively in order to come up with a plan for their contribution to the overall plan.

Meanwhile you will be ensuring that Q4 and 5 are addressed by those to whom you have given direction:

Question 4 – Where in the environment can I best achieve each action/effect?

In this case, as those to whom you have given direction provide you with the information from their analysis and reconnaissance, you can confirm that you are content that what has been provided in response to your direction gives you the information needed to select the best of the options suggested for each of the objectives that you have set.

Question 5 – What resources do I need for each action/effect?

The principal resources required in this situation are people and their skills. You make a judgment and brief those people who arrive, asking if they can help and where their help is needed having asked or been told of any relevant skills that they have; such as 'I am a nurse' or 'I am a mechanic'. You are deploying your assets to task.

Question 6 – When and where do the actions and effects need to take place in relation to each other?

This question could be 'what is the priority order of the effects that you have identified'. The priority order would probably be as shown in the table below:

Priority	Action	Who	When	Where	Remarks
1	Stop Traffic to protect the site.	Me and anyone who arrives from other directions	Immediately	In a safe place at each approach to the site	
2	Gather information before ringing 999 in order to ensure that you ask for the right services. Ring 999	Me	As soon as possible	Crash site	
3	Identify a safe place for the injured and give First Aid and reassurance	Me, anyone who is First Aid trained	Once 999 called and site is stable	Safe place (or if someone is trapped in a vehicle they will have to stay in the vehicle).	

Priority	Action	Who	When	Where	Remarks
4	Establish an Incident Control Point.	Me	Once 999 called and site is stable	Layby, field or an area within the stabilized site	
5	Any actions to help the injured and to prepare for the arrival of the emergency service.	All those who have offered help	Continual until Police arrive	Crash site, where safe	
6	Brief emergency services and follow instructions	Me	As emergency services arrive	Incident Control Point	

The table is a mental picture of what you might be thinking.

Question 7 – What Governance Measures do I need to establish.

The governance measures issued by you and anyone taking the lead in the Groups may include:

- Everyone arriving at the scene to be briefed before entering the site

- Nobody to enter the site unless they have a useful contribution to make.

- Routes into the site to be kept clear in order to enable easy access for the emergency services.

- No potential evidence to be removed or tampered with unless it is necessary so to do in support of saving life.

The emergency services will issue more control measures once they have taken over the situation.

SUMMARY

This chapter has aimed to show you in a logical way how planning, problem solving and decision making may take place in a very short timeframe. The questions would have been addressed intuitively and instinctively. The way in which the situation has been handled before the arrival of the emergency services would be dependent on the knowledge, experience and training of those involved and time.

The key points to take away from this chapter is that the 7 Questions provide a generic framework for thinking, which helps to order the thoughts that will be going through your mind in such a situation. If you can discipline your thinking to address the 'what and the why' before the 'how' in any such situation, it will eradicate many mistakes that could be made by diving straight into the 'how'. It will reduce the likelihood of having to go back to the beginning because your actions have been carried out in the wrong order.

For example in this situation if you were in such a hurry to get involved in dealing with those affected by the crash, you would risk making the situation worse; another vehicle might crash into yours if your 4 way flashers weren't switched on; and if you didn't dial 999 before you dived in to help the arrival of the emergency services would be delayed and lives might be lost rather than saved.

I have attempted to show you how the framework for thinking provided by 7 simple questions should be addressed in a way disciplined by the stages:

- Stage 1 - 'what and why' followed by:

- Stage 2 - 'gathering information and conducting analysis' before

- Stage 3 - 'the how',

will lead to more effective and less risky solutions to problems.

CHAPTER 4

STRATEGIC/DELIBERATE PLANNING

INTRODUCTION

Strategy is a plan of action designed to achieve a long-term or overall aim. Alternatively strategy is a plan to change the direction of an organisation due to a change in the environment and would address the resources required to enable the change in relation to its current markets, its customers or clients in order to optimize the benefit of the change. Brexit is a clear example of such a change in environment and will necessitate continual adjustments over the next few years due to the likelihood that the business environment may be subject to continual change.

The principles and approach to producing a strategic/deliberate plan or a project plan for more complex and larger scale projects are the same as they are for short term, intuitive planning. The big difference is that the tools, processes and level of research and analysis used to address each of the 7 Questions need to be commensurate with the complexity of the organisation/ project.

The 7 Questions approach does not necessarily change the tools and processes that are currently used, but is the framework for thinking, if applied effectively, can bring precision, organisation, order and discipline to the production of the plan and its supporting plans.

AIM

The aim of this chapter is to show how the 7 Questions can be used as the focus for the planning processes that you currently use in order to help you to conduct your current processes more efficiently and effectively.

A NEW APPROACH

A strategy needs to be set in the context of the new environment/situation, and set out a business's future outcomes and strategies for achieving them. The 7 Questions provide a logical framework for such a plan.

CONTEXT - ENVIRONMENTAL ANALYSIS

Before looking at how the changes in the business environment affect your business it is important to understand what is going on in the remote environment; that is the operational external environment. A common tool that can be used for this analysis is PEST or Political, Economic, Social. Technical analysis.

Political/Legal	Economic
Social/Cultural	Technical

7 QUESTIONS TO DEVELOP A STRATEGIC/DELIBERATE PLAN

Question 1

What are the issues (resulting from changes in my business environment) and why?

To address this question it is necessary to understand how the PEST analysis above affects your business environment, and why it will affect the business environment that you have based your current strategy on; that is the operational internal environment. The issues and opportunities as they affect your business in each of the functional areas should be analysed. This is a chance to involve each functional lead, or as an entrepreneur the functional areas you need to consider. It is suggested that you bring in the functional leads and involve them in the development of the strategy, to do the analysis from their perspective at the strategic level:

➢ Marketing and Sales

- The sales environment/market place

- Competitors and information about their reaction to the business environmental changes

➢ Personnel/HR

- The labour market

- Organizational structure

- Employment law

- Cultural effects and any need for change

➢ Finance

- VAT

- Tax

- Tariffs

- Costs/Prices

- Borrowing and cash flow analysis

- ➢ Supplies/resources

  - Buyers

  - Storage

  - Stock levels

- ➢ Manufacture

  - Infrastructure and facilities

  - Inventory required to meet orders on time.

  - Transport

  - Customs and supporting paperwork requirements

  - Tariffs

  - Traffic

- ➢ Business Development

  - Issues to be addressed to mitigate weaknesses and exploit opportunities.

- ➢ Information Technology

  - New requirements to mitigate the impact of issues identified.

- ➢ The law

- ➢ Health and safety

The list above is indicative but not appropriate for every business. There will be overlaps between functional areas and these need to be identified early to prevent functional leads working in silos and to integrate the contributions of each function.

A SWOT analysis can help to capture the detail of the issues your business must address. The results of the SWOT analysis can capture the issues that need to be included and addressed as you develop your strategy.

Advantages	Vulnerabilities
Strengths	Weaknesses
Opportunities	Threats

The key to addressing question 1 is to understand how the problems that a change in the business environment or the business environment you are planning to launch into, will affect your business and why. You should use whatever tools suit you to analyse the issues and to identify the 'why'; i.e. how the impact will affect your business if you do not plan how to overcome it.

It is important to start the development of a strategy by looking at Question 1 first to ensure that the Strategy is developed in the context of the issues and their impact; otherwise there is a risk of developing a flawed strategy that will not survive the impact of the issues on it. In the military our 'Estimate' process used to start with Mission Analysis before considering the enemy. This led the planners, (the Commander and Staff), to start the development of a plan in their minds without due consideration of 'what the enemy were doing and why'. This often led to false assumptions that were difficult to undo.

I suggest that, unless you have a business intelligence department within your organizational structure, the marketing and sales teams lead on this as they   are the team responsible for knowing what is going on in your market space/business environment. In addition everyone needs to think and report opportunities and threats and report their thoughts.

Question 2

What have I been told to do and why (or if you are the business owner what do I want to achieve and why)?

In the Army this question is addressed through a process that the British had adopted from the US Army called Mission Analysis. The process addressed 4 questions:

1.   What is my higher commander's intent?

2.   What are my specified tasks, implied tasks and purpose (my contribution to the higher commander's intent)?

3.   What constraints on my freedom of action have been imposed?

4.   If the Situation you based your strategy on has changed, consider 'How has the situation changed and why does it affect my strategy?'

The purpose of Question 2 is to ensure that you are absolutely clear on what you have been asked to do, or what you want to do if you are an entrepreneur, and that you understand the reason or the outcome your boss wants you to achieve to support his/her plan. If you are the boss running your own business you need to make a plan to achieve your mission to yourself, and have a clear vision of what you want to achieve and why.

Question 3

What outcomes/changes do I need to achieve (to address the effects of the changes to the business environment) and what information do I need to gather to make a plan?

Addressing Question 3 and producing an intent schematic showing the desired outcome for each contributory change will be the focus for developing the strategy. A brainstorming session with the appropriate directors and managers is a good way to get their buy in to the changes that are agreed.

An 'Intent Schematic' shows the desired outcomes and how they are linked to, and affect, each other and the contribution each functional area will make. It is the culmination of the 'What and why'. When it comes to addressing Questions 4 – 7, 'The How', there may be several ways that each outcome can be achieved; this will result in presenting to the leader each course of action, so that he/she can make a decision on the chosen course of action once Questions 4 – 7 have been addressed for each.

Intent Schematic:

Links made to new markets in the new trading environment in order to prepare the ground for new trade deals	◄——►	International lawyers engaged to oversee the drafting of trade deals in order to protect us

The changes to our new business environment matched to the business's capabilities and organizational changes made in order help the business to continue to succeed in the next decade

Organizational restructuring completed in order to enable us to exploit the new business environment.

Note: 1. The lines show that each outcome contributes to the overall desired outcome 2. This is illustrative and not linked to any scenario nor complete

Information requirements

1. New business environment needs constant monitoring to identify any developments.

2. Potential new markets need to be identified and PEST and/or SWOT analysis completed on each and legal implications identified.

3. Legal requirements for each new market/country.

4. What are the competition doing? This needs constant monitoring.

5. Note: the more complex the Strategy the more information requirements and analysis could be necessary to enable the addressing the 'How' Questions 4 - 7. Doing this work now will save you from going back to find out information and disturbing the flow of the planning of the 'How'.

THE HOW

If the addressing of Questions 1 - 3 has been done well, addressing Questions 4 - 7 will be much easier. There may be several potential Courses of Action for different ways to complete Questions 4 – 7; if that is the case you can complete them for each. The boss will then analyse each and decide upon the chosen COA.

Question 4

Where in the business environment can I best achieve each action and outcome?

From the completed Intent Schematic you need to plan where you want to make changes to achieve outcomes. E.g. For new markets it may be in another country and for organizational changes it may be both internal and external. Also note that you will need actions to achieve outcomes and hence actions and outcomes are included in Questions 4, 5 and 6.

Question 5

What resources do I need to achieve each action and outcome/change?

In addressing this question you need to consider all required resources; financial, human, equipment, software/IT etc. If you work for a large to medium size business you may need to explain the means and resources you need to achieve the required outcomes in a business plan to present to your governing body.

If you do not have enough resources for all the outcomes, you may need to take a risk by under-resourcing an outcome; the risk should be recorded in a risk management table. This must be monitored so that action can be taken if necessary.

You may need to produce a Business Plan to justify the resources you need.

Question 6

When and where do the actions and outcomes need to happen in relation to each other?

The table reflects in time and space the implementation of the plan. It needs to be monitored as the plan unfolds.

Integration/Synchronization Matrix				
Dates	Jan 2020 – Dec 2021	Jan 2021 – Dec 2022	Jan – Dec 2022	Jan 2023 to Jan 2030
Issues	Business environment changing	Current sales in current markets will not sustain the business	Issues to be discussed as they arise and plan adjusted accordingly.	Issues to be discussed as they arise and plan adjusted accordingly.
Actions/ Outcomes	Make links with potential new markets	Potential new markets identified	Plan for moving into new markets agreed by the Board	New plan implemented by all departments
Marketing	Find potential new markets	Identify the implications of moving into each new marketing area to inform decision making on 'go no go'.	Launch your new products on the markets	
Sales	Gather intelligence on the potential of new markets	Plan how best to sell the new products	Start selling the products	
HR		Analyze HR Implications of establishing new markets		
Operations		Analyze the operational implications of new markets	Lead on the plan for the establishment of new markets and the move into new areas of operation with all functional leads	
Manufacture	Analyze the implications of new or adjusted product for new markets			
Logistics		Analyze the logistical implications of potential new markets	Ensure the required inventory is in place to exploit new markets	
Finance		Analyze the cost of moving into new markets and the pricing structures for each		

Question 7

What governance measures need to be imposed (without unnecessarily restricting freedom of action)?

Governance measures need to be imposed in order to keep the planning and implementation of the plan synchronized and integrated. The CEO needs to be reassured that the planning and implementation of the Strategy is going in the right direction and that he/she is informed of issues that cannot be resolved at departmental level. He/she does not need to get involved in the detail and he/she needs to empower departmental heads. If he/she is concerned about a department he/she may need to keep a closer eye on it by imposing some extra governance measures on the leader. If the CEO interferes and shows lack of trust in any department to function as required he/she will give a negative feeling to their department. The CEO needs to trust his departmental heads until they prove he/she cannot and then appropriate action needs to be imposed.

Summary

I have tried to show how the 7 Questions can be used at the Strategic or Operational level. They are a framework for thinking and can be applied to any level of planning. They are not a process; processes can, and may need, to be used, where appropriate to address each Question. In a crisis situation they provide a logical approach to making a quick plan to deal with the situation.

General Sir Mike Jackson, when he was Commander-in-Chief Land Command, at a Command meeting, is reported to have taken a copy of the 7 Questions out of his pocket and said 'have you heard about the 7 Questions? They are what I needed when I got to Pristina Airport' (to find the Russians already there). At that stage the military version of the 7 Questions was a proposal and not agreed by the Joint Services Doctrine Centre. It went on to approve them to be taught from Corporal to Brigadier. I hope you find the business version helpful and that they are adaptable to all levels of responsibility.

CHAPTER 5

Scenarios and Examples

When I had developed the 7 Questions for the military, a colleague of mine briefed a business man friend of his on them and in response he sent me a copy of the Goal[1].

First Example of Using the 7 Questions

The Goal makes the point very well. The book is a fiction with a really powerful business message; a manufacturing plant is losing money and the Corporate Vice President has threatened the manager with closure unless he turns around the plant into a profit making asset within 3 months. The Goal shows how important Questions 1, 2 and 3 are to the development of a strategy to drive your business in the right direction, one that results in success.

I will now use the 7 Questions, loosely using the Goal, as a worked example in the context that you can adapt to your own business.

Context

The Plant is visited by the Vice President from Company Head Office who turns up unexpectedly early one morning to see Alex, the plant manager, before he gets in to work; he starts to stop the work that was going on and tells everyone to work on an order that was overdue, following a complaint to the Head Office. Alex's managers are furious because they had spent hours setting up the machines for another order. In the rush caused by the anger of the Vice President a machine operator forgets to complete the setting up task correctly and breaks the machine. In the angry response to this delay the machine operator resigned and walked

1   *The Goal by Elyahu M Goldratt and Jeff Cox*
www.tocinstitute.org/the-goal-summary.htmlex

out leaving his foreman to fix the machine. This is the situation facing Alex when he enters his office.

Alex angrily challenges the Vice President and in the ensuing discussion Alex is told that the plant will be closed after 3 months unless it stops making a loss. Alex has no idea why the plant is making a loss as all the measurements on the productivity and efficiencies of the plant that he sends to Head Office are good.

To cut a long story short Alex is flying to a meeting at Head Office and meets his Physics Professor, Jonah, from his College days and tells him about the problem. In response Jonah asks lots of questions and left Alex to think about what the Goal of his plant was. Following a phone call later to try to make sense of the 3 measurements that Jonah advised Alex what to measure to establish why the plant is making a loss; they are inventory (material held and being processed) throughput (work in process to meet orders), and operating costs. Armed with this guidance Alex starts to make a plan with the help of his managers.

Question 1: What are the issues and why?

- The plant is not making money and will be closed if the plant isn't turned around.

- The warehouse is full of inventory of material needed to keep the whole plant working at full capacity 24/7; this has caused piles of inventory waiting to be processed at two of the machines

- Another warehouse is holding products that the plant has produced but hasn't sold

- The measurements he sends to Head Office do not measure the plant's profitability/loss making figures, but productivity and efficiency that shows that everyone is working all the time making a lot of products;

not all these products contribute to meeting orders on time.

Question 2: What have I been told to do and why?

To turn the plant around to meet orders on time in order to make the plant profitable.

Specified tasks:

1. To change the operating model of the plant to meet orders on time.

2. To make the plant profitable

Implied tasks:

1. To identify bottlenecks.

2. To reduce inventory to what is needed to meet orders.

3. To govern the release of inventory to meet the speed at which the bottlenecks can process it.

4. To sell finished products that have been made and held in a warehouse at cost or a small profit

Question 3: What changes/outcomes do I need to make to overcome the issues and what information do I need to make to develop a plan?

The Intent Schematic that I have developed from The Goal illustrates what a valuable tool it is. It can help you to direct your team to plan each of the changes. If you have read the Goal you will be able to understand how helpful this framework for thinking can be.

Intent Schematic:

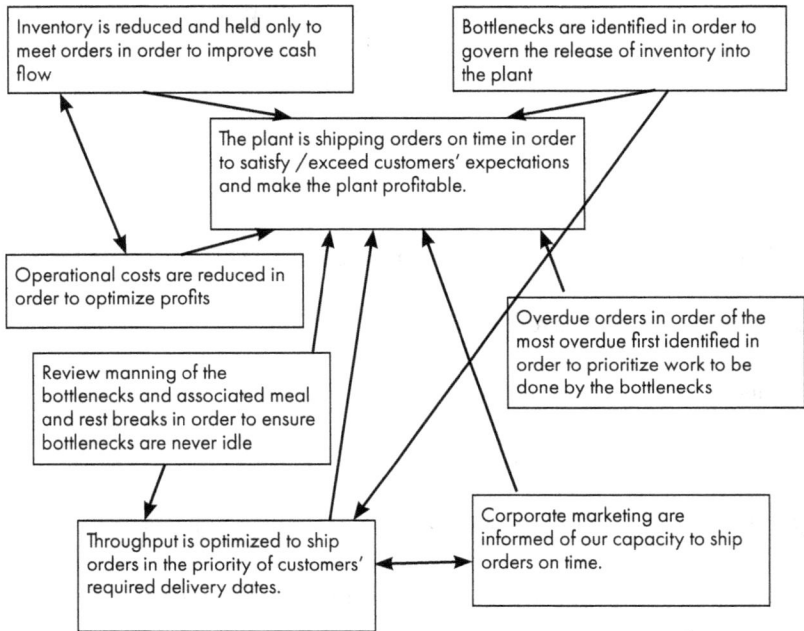

Inventory is reduced and held only to meet orders in order to improve cash flow

Bottlenecks are identified in order to govern the release of inventory into the plant

The plant is shipping orders on time in order to satisfy / exceed customers' expectations and make the plant profitable.

Operational costs are reduced in order to optimize profits

Review manning of the bottlenecks and associated meal and rest breaks in order to ensure bottlenecks are never idle

Overdue orders in order of the most overdue first identified in order to prioritize work to be done by the bottlenecks

Throughput is optimized to ship orders in the priority of customers' required delivery dates.

Corporate marketing are informed of our capacity to ship orders on time.

Note: The lines show that each change/outcome contributes to the achievement of the Goal and the inter-dependence between changes/outcomes

Information requirements:

1. Orders pending in priority order.

2. Completed products not required for orders to be available for sale

3. What are the plant's bottlenecks and how long does it take to set them up for, and process parts?

4. What parts do not require to be processed by bottlenecks?

5.   How are the bottlenecks staffed?

Questions 4 – 7. The How?

I suggest that you read The Goal and you could use it as a training exercise for your team by reviewing what I have written for Questions 1 - 3 and then ask them to complete Questions 4 - 7; or you can use it to develop your own strategy.

Question 4: Where in the business environment (the plant) does each action and change need to take place?

Question 5: What resources are required to achieve each action and change/outcome?

Question 6: When and where do the actions and changes/outcomes need to happen in relation to each other?

Synchronization and Integration (or Synergy) Matrix

Date/Time								
Issues								
Actions/Changes								
Who to action								

This table reflects the plan to achieve the Goal and would be a dynamic documents that will need adapting as actions taken impact on the system.

Question 7: What governance measures do I need to impose?

You will realise that the governance measures (the reports that need to be completed and sent to HQ) have been counter-productive and new measures need to be implemented. The three operational measurements recommended by Jonah are; **Throughput** is the rate at which the system generates money through sales; **Inventory** is all the material that the system is processing to meet orders; **Operational expense** is all the cash the system spends in order to turn inventory into throughput to meet orders on time.

Second Example

Context

When I was working in the MOD I found that using Questions 1 – 3 were a most useful agenda to get issues resolved; for example:

I was responsible for ensuring that the non-equipment lines of development were addressed for the project to procure the first tactical digital communication system for operations and training for those using the communication system in a Headquarters from the lowest level, section, up the chain of command to battlegroup headquarters and from there to Brigade HQ.

I identified that in barracks training on the digital radios and the incorporated applications had not been included in the procurement of the system. So I called a meeting with all the key players to find a solution.

Question 1: What are the issues and why?

The need to train on the new radio system and its incorporated applications had been considered but not addressed.

The assumption that a network could be set up in barracks for training was not practicable.

The need for licenses to be procured for training in barracks has not been addressed.

Question 2: What do I want to achieve and why?

I want to address the need to train in barracks in order to enable Headquarters staff to train on the applications as part of their training before deployment on training and operations.

Question 3: What outcomes do I need to achieve and what information do I need to develop a plan?

Intent Schematic

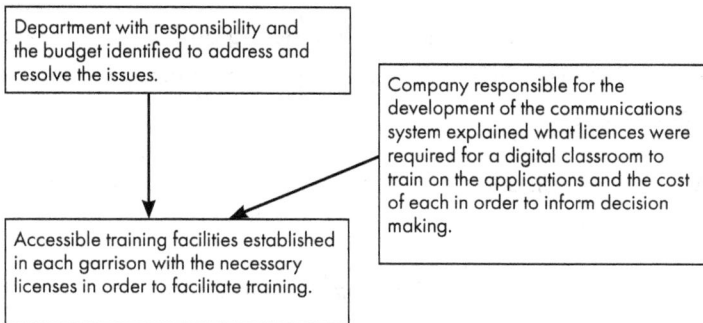

Department with responsibility and the budget identified to address and resolve the issues.

Company responsible for the development of the communications system explained what licences were required for a digital classroom to train on the applications and the cost of each in order to inform decision making.

Accessible training facilities established in each garrison with the necessary licenses in order to facilitate training.

By using Questions 1 – 3 I was able the hand over the responsibility to the appropriate department. I then learned that my job in a large and complex government department was not to solve issues but to get them solved.

The department with the responsibility and budget took on addressing Q 4 – 7 and the classrooms are now in place.

Third Example

Context

When I left the Army in 2009 I was selected for a job as Head of an Activity Centre. I was brought in as the first Head of Centre. I spent, my first month finding out about how the operations at the Centre worked and identifying the issues affecting its performance. Over the next 10 years all have been resolved and the Centre makes an operational profit. .It is much leaner and makes an operational profit.

Question 1: What are the issues and why?

- Customer focus is haphazard before during and after each booking which affects repeat bookings and reputation due to lack of a Centre Manager.

- Management of, and accounting for, activity equipment is poor due to the lack of a nominated lead.

- Lack of financial information from the North Yorkshire Youth head office to Carlton Lodge Activity Centre is not in place because of the lack of integration and communication between the two offices and no Centre Manager.

- Tidiness of Reception and public areas give customers a bad impression.

- There is no formal marketing lead for the Activity Centre leading to missed opportunities for optimizing the potential of the Centre

- There is no development plan nor lead for optimizing the Centre grounds for additional activities.

- Facilities attract negative comments and could put customers off return visits.

- No regular meetings of managers leads to mistakes in the synchronization and integration in managing the delivery of bookings.

Question 2: What do I have I been told to achieve and why?

To take responsibility for the development and delivery of the programmes and activities of the Centre in order to turn it into a beacon of excellence in providing day and residential programmes of adventurous activities to support the education and development of children and young people.

Question 3: What changes and outcomes do I need to achieve and what information do I need to develop a plan?

This Intent Schematic was a reflection of what was done over my time as Head of Centre and required close cooperation with the Deputy Chief Executive (who became Chief Executive) and my managers. Knowledge and ideas sharing up and down the chain of command to optimize the potential of the Centre and build up relationships of trust and mutual understanding was essential.

Intent Schematic

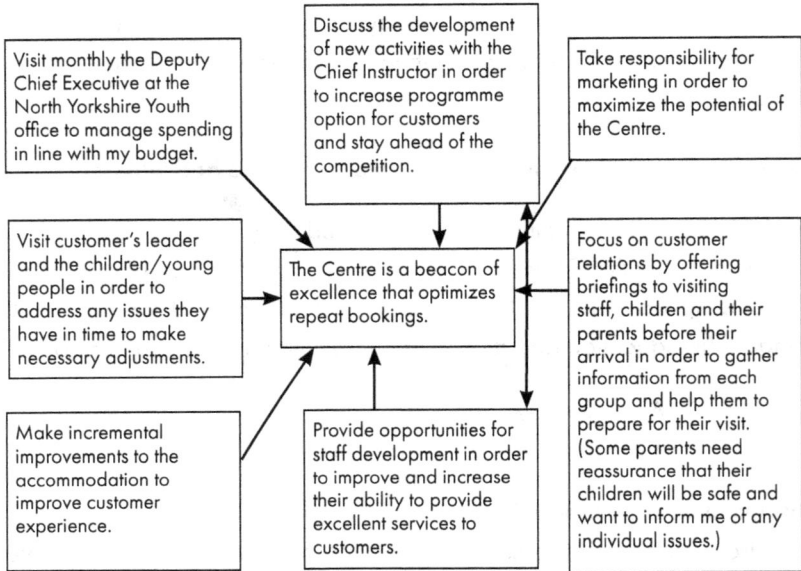

Visit monthly the Deputy Chief Executive at the North Yorkshire Youth office to manage spending in line with my budget.

Discuss the development of new activities with the Chief Instructor in order to increase programme option for customers and stay ahead of the competition.

Take responsibility for marketing in order to maximize the potential of the Centre.

Visit customer's leader and the children/young people in order to address any issues they have in time to make necessary adjustments.

The Centre is a beacon of excellence that optimizes repeat bookings.

Focus on customer relations by offering briefings to visiting staff, children and their parents before their arrival in order to gather information from each group and help them to prepare for their visit. (Some parents need reassurance that their children will be safe and want to inform me of any individual issues.)

Make incremental improvements to the accommodation to improve customer experience.

Provide opportunities for staff development in order to improve and increase their ability to provide excellent services to customers.

Question 4. Where in the environment can I best achieve each action and effect?

All the actions and effects can take place within the Centre except:

- Courses for staff will take place at the course provider's location.

- Pre visit briefings to customers will take place at their location

- Off-site adventurous activities

- Meetings with the CEO and his deputy.

Question 5. What assets do I need for each action and effect?

All actions/effects are cost neutral except:

- The cost of training courses needs to be briefed to the Chief Executive to confirm that they are within my training budget or ask for the extra funding as soon as possible.

- Travel costs to events/meetings/visits to customers pre visit unless within my budget.

- Marketing material.

- Improvement to accommodation; I need to apply to trusts, foundations or District/County Council.

Before each financial year I need to discuss my budget requirements for the following year to ask for them to be included in the next year's budget. For this I need to have a compelling case.

Question 6. When and where do the actions/effects need to happen in relation to the others?

Target Date	Immediate	Immediate	Years 1 - 10	Years 1 - 10	Years 1 - 10	Years 1 - 10
Issues	Build stronger customer relationships	Lack of communication with Head Office and within the Centre	Limited activities	Lack of opportunity for staff dev.	No one responsible for marketing	Facilities attract negative comments
Head of Centre	Visit customer's leader and group	Meet Deputy CEO monthly to discuss funding issues. And establish a weekly team meeting with all managers.		Discuss Budget for courses and get them in the budget year on year		
Bookings Manager					Take responsibility for sales & marketing	
Chief Instructor			Develop new activities on and off-site and bid to head of Centre for funds	Conduct a training needs analysis to identify courses or on-site training.		
Facilities Manager						Identify costed improvement to accommodation in priority order for the Head of Centre
Senior Instructor / Head of Centre			Year 5 Appoint a permanent Senior Instructor to line manage seasonal instructors and take responsibility for equipment care and personal protective equipment			

Remarks: on reflection over the last 10 years all of the issues have been addressed and the Centre has been turned around due to excellent team work and great help and support from the Deputy and now CEO. I moved on from my post without any skeletons in the cupboard! The Framework for thinking has become an intuitive way of analysing and either resolving or getting issues resolved.

Question 7. What Governance Measures do I need to impose (without unnecessarily restricting Freedom of Action)?

The most important and effective Governance Measures are:

- The weekly Team Meeting. This meeting always addressed any issues from the current and previous week's bookings, the bookings for the next 2 weeks in detail and the bookings for the following 3 weeks in general. This ensured that the whole team was integrated and the activity, accommodation and feeding were synchronised and the managers had the information they needed. I also asked for updates and issues from each manager's areas. It also gave the managers a chance to question me and ask for direction.

- My monthly meetings at the North Yorkshire Youth office and with the Deputy Chief Executive kept me in touch with what was going on in the rest of the organisation and to get updated and given direction on spending and to ask for funds in future months I could also raise issues and ask for advice or direction

- Finally, my daily visits to the leaders of each group gave them and me a chance to raise issue as appropriate. That made the customers feet that we were there to help them to get what they wanted from their time with us and for me to develop good customer relations and a relationship of trust and mutual understanding.

Summary

I hope that you can see that the 7 Questions is a Framework for Thinking when you are making a plan Hastily/Intuitively (in your mind) or Deliberately for addressing and making a plan for a complex situation. It is an approach rather than a process. I hope that this approach is a 'Generic Improved Framework for Thinking'.

You will have seen from the Forward that Professor Panos Louvieris has adopted the 7 Questions for his research projects. He was very quick to recognise the value of this approach for any problem.